The CHRISTMAS STORY

In Reading, Verse & Carol

Olive Sharpe.

MOORLEY'S Print & Publishing

Publishers of Christian Books ——————— Printers
* Copying & Duplicating * Commercial Stationery *

<u>Congregational Hymn</u>	"Love came down at Christmas"
<u>Prayer</u>	
<u>Scripture Reading</u>	Isaiah Ch. 9 verses 1-7

****

Poem (1)	"Promised"
Scripture Reading	St. Matthew Ch. 1 v 18-23
Congregational Hymn	"Hark the glad sound"
Scripture Reading	St. Luke Ch. 2 v 1-7
Poems (2) and (3)	"The Journey"
	"The Stable"
Children's Hymn	"Once in royal David's city"
Scripture Reading	St. Luke Ch. 2 v 8-14
Poems (4) and (5)	"The Shepherds"
	"The Reason Why"
Congregational Hymn	"Hark! the herald angels sing"
Scripture Reading	St. Luke Ch. 2 v 15 - 16
Poems (6) and (7)	"Let Us Go"
	"The Baby"
Children's Hymn	"Away in a manger"
Congregational Hymn	"O come all ye faithful"
Scripture Reading	St. Matthew Ch. 2 v 1-12
Poem (8)	"The Wise Men"
Congregational Hymn	"As with gladness"
Poem (9)	"What Will <u>You</u> Say?"
Congregational Hymn	"Thou didst leave Thy Throne"
Benediction	

POEM (1)

"Promised"

How easily we promise things on every passing
day!
And at the time, we truly mean to do the thing
we say;
But other tasks come crowding in, and other
people too
May sometimes make impossible, the thing we
planned to do:
And at the closing of the day, the weary sigh
is heard,
"I promised I would do it, but I had to break
my word!"
How deeply grateful we should be, with God
'tis never so!
No power in heaven or earth can change the
thing He plans to do.
And when He makes a promise, then that promise
is fulfilled,
The very place, the day, the hour, is just as
He has willed.
Long years ago, He promised that a little
child should come,
Should weep, and laugh, and play and grow, and
make the earth His home.
But, as He grew, men would discern this was no
common child,
The sins that spoiled them everyone, would
leave Him undefiled.

Till, when He came to man's estate, on one
                    dark, dreadful day,
He would be nailed upon a cross, to bear man's
                    sin away.
For He would be no other than God's well-
                    beloved Son
Who, from the dawning of the age, had made
                    man's cause His own.
..... God had not said <u>when</u> He would come, so,
                    down the centuries,
The faithful few watched for His day, with
                    patient, wistful eyes.
<u>They</u> slept, and others kept the watch, hearts
                    torn with hope and fear:
Till, slowly, earth's great moment struck -
                    the promised time was here!

****

Scripture Reading   St. Matthew Ch. 1   v 18-23

Congregational Hymn   "Hark the glad sound"

Scripture Reading   St. Luke Ch. 2 v 1-7

POEM (2)

"The Journey"

    "From Nazareth to Bethlehem" -
How <u>long</u> the journey seemed to them!
They could not travel far each day,
And few the inns where they could stay;
And often, they would have to rest
In cheerless places, cramped, and pressed.
So <u>many</u> travellers were bound
Like Joseph, for their native ground,
To pay their tax like honest men,
And then, to travel back again.
If rough and sordid was the place,
And pinched and pale was Mary's face,
Then, Joseph told her tenderly,
"The Bethlehem folk are known to me,
I know the inn - they'll take you there,
And you can rest without a care".
Poor Joseph! - little did he know
The town was full to overflow!
The inn he knew in days of yore
Was turning <u>rich</u> men from the door!
The night was falling steadily,
And Mary's plight was plain to see.
With anguished eyes he looked around,
<u>Some</u> kind of shelter must be found:
The stables! - would he - <u>could</u> he dare
To take his wife to shelter there?

- 5 -

POEM (3) -- A fancy

"The Stable"

I hope they swept the stables <u>clean</u>
The little boys of Bethlehem!
Grand folk would come, with beasts they
                        prized,
And maybe notice them!
I hope they made the mangers sweet,
Brushed with a will, the hard, rough,
                        wood,
It might mean gifts, or even <u>pence</u>!
Rich folk were sometimes good.
But who, I wonder, swept the stall
Where Joseph came, at close of day,
With Mary clinging to his arm
And sank amongst the hay?
<u>They</u> had no gifts to offer him,
Yet <u>how</u> I hope the little lad
Ran to his home that winter night
His heart made strangely glad.
And, in the days when he was old,
I like to think men heard him say,
"<u>I</u> swept the stall where, first of all
My own dear Saviour lay!"

****

Children's Hymn   "Once in royal David's
                        City."

- 6 -

POEM (4)

"The Shepherds"

The sheep, within the rough stone wall,
    were resting peacefully,
The great fire, kindled by the door,
    was burning cheerily,
Around it lay the shepherds
    of the safely-folded sheep,
One keeping watch, while others dozed,
    or sank in dreamless sleep.
The lights of crowded Bethlehem
    shone out across the night;
And surely, never had the stars seemed
    quite so large and bright!
The stars? - no! - these were never stars!
    The watcher raised his eyes,
The heavens above were all ablaze:
    "Arise!" he cried, "arise!"
The sleepers woke in terror, and rose,
    stumbling to their feet,
Then gasped, as, high above their heads,
    a voice spoke, clear and sweet.
"Fear not! - I bring you tidings
    of a joy unknown before,
A joy that shall embrace the world,
    and stretch from shore to shore!
To you is born in Bethlehem,
    a Saviour, Christ the Lord;
And so that you may prove it true,
    God sends this special word:
You will not find the infant Christ
    in any princely hall,
But wrapped in coarsest linen bands,
    laid in a cattle stall!"

The shepherds raised their dazzled eyes
        in wonder, to behold
The heavens filled with the angel hosts,
        on wings of shining gold.
All chanting sweetly as they came,
        again, and yet again,
"To God be all the glory,
        and goodwill and peace to men!"

POEM (5)

"The Reason Why"

I wonder why God chose to tell the shepherds
        first of all
About the new Messiah, in the humble cattle
        stall?
I think perhaps, He knew these men who had
        to spend their days
In leading sheep to pasture-lands, through
        rough and dangerous ways,
Who could not keep the Festivals, nor yet the
        Sabbath day,
Because they had to guard their flocks from
        prowling beasts of prey;
Might well have feared the Christ who came,
        was not for such as they,
But only for the pious folk, with time to
        fast and pray!
And so, He sent a special word, to tell them
        it was true
The new-born Christ of Bethlehem had come to
        save them, too!

That, just as they would leave their sheep –
      with others – in the fold,
To seek a lost one, wandering out in the
      dark and cold,
So He had come to seek for them, the lonely
      and unsought,
As much as for the busy crowds, that thronged
      the temple court!

****

Congregational Hymn   "Hark! the herald angels
                           sing"

Scripture Reading   St. Luke Ch. 2 v 15-16

POEM (6)

"Let Us Go"

How dark the night, without a light
Save from the flickering fire!
How cold and still, the field and hill
Without the angel choir!
Still in a daze, the shepherds gaze
Where late the angels soared:
Till one spoke low, "Come, let us go
And seek our infant Lord!"
Their needed sleep – unguarded sheep
All vanish from their mind!
They hasten down toward the town
The infant Christ to find.
How did they know just where to go?
How could they find the way?
God their feet where; small and sweet,
The new-born Baby lay.

POEM (7)

"The Baby"

Half eagerly, half fearfully, they halted at
        the door,
Who should be first to raise the latch, and
        cross the stable floor?
For everyone had sinned and failed - yes
        every single one,
No one was worthy to approach God's own
        beloved Son!
Then, one aged shepherd whispered low,
        amongst the shadows dim,
"Come friends, and let us enter, for He bade
        us come to Him!"
.... How small He was! How sweet He was!
        there in His manger bed!
Where, in the morn, as every day, the
        cattle would be fed.
The shepherds, as they gathered round, lost
        all their guilty fears,
But, as they gazed, their tired eyes were
        filled with sudden tears.
Rough hands, that wielded every day, the
        crook, the staff, the sword,
Were clasped in worship, as they knelt
        before their infant Lord:
Then, tenderly, with reverent lips, they
        kissed His tiny hand,
- They had not gifts - save but themselves -
        but He would understand!

****

Children's Hymn   "Away in a manger"

Congregational Hymn   "O come all ye faithful"

Scripture Reading   St. Matthew Ch.2 v 1-12

POEM (8)

"The Wise Men"

They came to quiet Bethlehem
Wise Men, from far away,
Led by a star that guided them
To where the Baby lay.
They brought Him frankincense and gold,
Myrrh from the forest tree,
All symbols of what life would hold,
And what His tasks would be.
Why did each bring so strange a thing?
Where was their native land?
Such things as these are mysteries
We may not understand.
But this we know, God bade them go,
And they at once obeyed;
Though many scorned, and others warned,
They followed, undismayed.
Wise men were they, the Scriptures say,
That came to Bethlehem.
And wise are we, whoe'er we be
Who follow after them!

****

Congregational Hymn   "As with gladness"

"What will you say?"

God kept the promise that He made long
                     centuries ago,
And sent the little Heavenly Child to this
                     sad world below.
Two thousand years have almost passed since,
                     on that wondrous night,
The little town of Bethlehem was bathed in
                     Heaven's own light.
But oh Christ did not come to bring a season
                     of good-will,
A time of gifts and greetings, and a
                     children's Festival!
He came to bring Salvation to a world of
                     needy men,
Salvation that we need today, as much as
                     they did then.
He wants to dwell within our hearts, transform
                     them by His grace,
Just as He turned a cattle-shed into a holy
                     place.
He comes to you this Christmas, seeking still
                     an earthly home;
What will you say? - "Lord, enter"? - or will
                     you say - "No room"?

****

Congregational Hymn   "Thou didst leave Thy
                            Throne"

BENEDICTION